Shoo,

For the real Rosie

Rosie liked most animals.
She liked cats and dogs.
She liked birds and frogs.
But she didn't like flies.

3

When she saw a fly,
she would say,
"Shoo, Fly, don't bother me.
Fly away and leave me be!"

4

But sometimes flies
landed on Rosie.
This always made her cry.

Her mother would say,
"How can a fly
make you cry?
Here's a fly swatter.
Give it a try."

But Rosie wouldn't hurt a fly. She tried to scare the flies away instead.

She played loud music.
That only scared away
her dad.

Rosie put a fan
near the front door
and turned it up high.

She wanted the fan to blow
the flies out of the house.
It only scared away her cat.

Rosie sang her
fly song loudly.

"Shoo, Fly, don't bother me.
Shoo, Fly, don't bother me.
Shoo, Fly, don't bother me.
Fly away and leave me be!"

The song only scared away
her dog.

She put water and lemon juice in a bottle, and sprayed it near the flies.

It only made her cat and dog sneeze.

15

Then Rosie had an idea.
She asked her mother
if there was anything
that would stop flies
from bothering her.

Her mother said there was
a plant that could help.
Then she smiled.

The next day, Rosie and her mother went to the garden store. Rosie asked for the plant that could stop flies from bothering her.

The man in the store
gave her a tiny plant.
It looked too little
to scare away a flea!

Rosie took the plant home.
She looked at it.
It didn't look scary.
She sniffed the plant.
It didn't smell horrible.

But, after the plant had
been in Rosie's bedroom
for a day, she didn't
see any more flies.

Rosie went to talk
to her mother.
"This is the best plant
in the world!"

Her mother smiled.
"Yes," she said. "It's called
a Venus flytrap!"

Venus Flytrap Facts

A Venus flytrap is
a plant that "eats"
flies and other insects.

Each leaf has three hairs on it.
When an insect lands on a leaf
and touches a hair, the leaf
shuts and traps the insect.